ever-crossings

ever-crossings

Bruce Kauffman

First Edition

Wet Ink Books
www.WetInkBooks.com
WetInkBooks@gmail.com

ever-crossings
by Bruce Kauffman

Cover Design – Richard M. Grove
Layout and Design – Richard M. Grove

Typeset in Aptos
Printed and bound in Canada
Distributed in USA by Ingram,
  – to set up an account – 1-800-937-0152

Library and Archives Canada Cataloguing in Publication

Title: Ever-crossings / Bruce Kauffman.
Names: Kauffman, Bruce, 1950- author.
Identifiers: Canadiana 20250315858 | ISBN 9781998324279 (softcover)
Subjects: LCGFT: Poetry.
Classification: LCC PS8621.A685 E94 2025 | DDC C811/.6—dc23

Being a Person

Be a person here. Stand by the river, invoke
the owls. Invoke winter, then spring.
Let any season that wants to come here make its own
call. After that sound goes away, wait.

A slow bubble rises through the earth
and begins to include sky, stars, all space,
even the outracing, expanding thought.
Come back and hear the little sound again.

Suddenly this dream you are having matches
everyone's dream, and the result is the world.
If a different call came there wouldn't be any
world, or you, or the river, or the owls calling.

How you stand here is important. How you
listen for the next things to happen. How you breathe.

– William Stafford
From: "Even in Quiet Places: Poems"
(Confluence Press, 2010)

Table of Contents

ever-crossings

once

once there was
        a day
        or a moment
        or a person
        a thing
so brilliant
so perfect
it could never
        happen again

and then it did

questions again

i ask questions
in the dark

alone

not even sure if
anyone is listening

i ask also
for breath

      and have been
      given that so far

so perhaps
      someone is

i too ask forgiveness
for my occasional sense
of not being enough

or too much

or of being lost
      when the way is
      and was clearly marked

to all those times
i have not heard
a response

perhaps it
        not needed

perhaps
        the breath

        enough

on writing poetry

you will not write
your best poems
      on paper

especially not
      a computer

you will seemingly
write those instead

with invisible ink
      on the backs of wild
      horses and ponies

or in a patterned
remnant of tea leaves
      on the feathered
      tail of a dove

or in coloured braille
      on the wings of
      a butterfly

      a dragonfly

those

those
are the poems
that will come back
      to you

each of them believing in you
as much as you
      believed in them

there was
a poetic fable

there was a time
before time

where there was
nothing

        except

        a small black dot

there in the centre
of a vast nothingness

until
that dot believed
it wanted to be more

there was no sight
        yet
hearing came first

that dot could hear
        a soft voice

                and yes, yes indeed

                even today
                dots can hear

                i mean even a period
                knows when a sentence
                ends   but

back to this
that soft voice said to the dot
and now too i give you sight
open your eyes

i have created a small
pool of a new thing
     let's call it water

and created it
     from nothing but
     two parts of air
look at yourself in it

the dot looked
saw only its tiny
black self

nothing else

there was nothing
beyond just the small pool
     in front of it
     holding within
     that dot's reflection

nothing else at all
     in front of
     around
     or behind

and so because it could hear
the dot asked that soft voice
     for music

               that music of colour
               that magic of time

and the soft voice said
    granted

and so you see
    there was no big
    bang

instead but the tiniest of
    spark
    barely a coloured flash

and
the universe
    became

reunion

and as it happens
you will arrive

you will come
          to me
on the edge
          of a day

i will sense it

i will hear
          your breath
long before i see
you
          walking along
          then toward me
on and from
an ever-horizon's path

today
          as you approach
i can see you now
carrying a tiny package

a compact square box

in it
you have placed
          a hand-sized parcel
                    of hope

you speak of it and say
      i found this yesterday

it was something
      then you say
you thought you'd lost
      and given up
      ever finding again

i place two fingers
on top of the box

i can feel the warmth
the fullness

      the pulse
      of what's within

i believe you know
      already
but i look at you
and confirm
      what's inside is
      indeed alive

this
this fragile thing
you hold in your
      hands
and near to you
ever-so careful to not
      let it drop

or be taken

get lost again

i tell you to keep it close

you smile

and up against
your chest you
pull it closer

you know already

some days

it will be
all you have

in our haste what we forget

i was sitting in a not crowded movie theatre
still waiting for the show to begin
the usual perfunctory screens of slogans
and messages about the lobby
      concession stand
      where the trash receptacles are
upcoming films and extra attractions
      when
off to the side, with the houselights now
quickly dimming
i watched someone come in
      and in this near dark now they
slow-walking their way up the aisle to their row

and what amazed me
that from their chest
      was a soft glowing light
      as if emanating from within

for several seconds i sat astonished
as that glow never went away
and out of the corner of my eye
i saw a youngish child also
watching that person
i looked over
said to them
      in just above a whisper
      did you see that light too

they turned to me as if almost
surprised that i would ask and said
yes i did   and i still do sir
just like i saw everyone else's
as they came in   yours too
i see it in everyone
and everything

just like everyone else does
        all the time

and then the child looking me
straight in the eye said
and i believe you sir
        used to see it
        that way too

that unknown

there was once
a thing
  that had no
  name

  discovered
    in a way

it was unique
one of a kind
  and obvious in that

people through
all the ages
  and languages
tried to ascribe
to fix a name to it

but anything affixed
would simply roll off
as if fluid
  or round

they even attempted
sometimes in general
to simply call it
  that

but too nebulous
even *that* soon
  fell away

people from all over
hearing about it
  its story
chased after it

seeking their own chance
        to look
        to see
and claim their own
word for
        and attach
        that to it

but this entity
this *thing*
growing weary of its
        notoriety
retreated

found solace
in the far reaches
        of the world

inside forests
or jungles

in a river's water
        or waterfall

the morning dew

in the cosmic film
just above and below
        and before
        a sunrise

inside deep caves
where only an ever-trickling
of water was all that
        could be heard

or
it would climb up
into the deepest part
        of the night

become the tiniest part
of a night sky

a tiny light
blending with stars

sometimes visible
sometimes not
in its blinking colours
            red
            burgundy
            green
            orange
            blue

it there anonymous
nearly always
            unnoticed
in its now obscurity

and seeming happiest
            there

this thing
still without
            a name

will never have one

can never have one

but it is that
            first breath

            or last

in that instant
            before
            wonder begins

we are

we are
not what we do

even less
what we say

we are the
conversations
        within us

no   not
the superficial
        monologues

but the deeper
dialogues

        between the
        halves

        those ever-two
        selves inside
                each of us

we are not
the legacies
        we believe we
        are
                or leave
                behind

after all
those fluid things
become
        diluted
        scattered

perhaps
it is not legacy
we should seek

but instead
        legitimacy
an ethics about us
an honesty
a compassion even

even in those times
        when it is less
                popular

        less easy

and really
in the end

in the all of life

truly
we are
        and become
        each
much more
        our dreams

        than our days

rails

westbound train
boarded this morning

no destination
no getting off

nearly a continent away
        taking it all the way
        to the west coast

i'm anonymous
a number
        ticket number
20 – via rail canada – economy –
car 4 – window – toronto to vancouver

that's
who i'll be
for the next few days

at least tens of thousands
of others have been
        the same
same name
        same seat, same train,
        same car, same ticket

i boarded alone
will ride this rail
        disembark
the same

this trip
isn't about
        people
just country
        landscapes

        the closeness of it

days of it
        4

                never considered
                the not-enough airplane
                with its glossy-cover-magazine-
                ride   showing
                        everything
                        and nothing

                its few hour long
                short expedition
                without heart
                        memoryless
                        after

                i need something
                        more

                want a trip that has
                        a pulse

i will disembark
on the west coast
stay
  maybe a day
  or two

then get back
on board
  come back

the whole way
again alone

  and
  not

for father again – a quarter century on

i'd never seen my father cry
in all the years i was a child
and even further on i
a young adult and then middle aged

in those days in that part of the world
most felt a man crying was
        a sign of weakness

even in his/those later years
and his failing health
        less mobile life

in it he able still to *get around* a bit
and able to fully talk and carry on
        long conversations

i did not see him once in it all
ever weep about his weakened
physical health or abilities

but during the christmas seasons
with christmas music filtering every year
in low volume throughout my parents' home
in his final two of those years
for a bit he would excuse himself
from the main room all of us were in
as he secured and positioned his cane
to go into the adjacent room and
sit beside the stereo there
whenever his favourite christmas
album would begin to play

and i would peek around the corner
of our room into the one he was in
        making sure he was okay
and he unaware i was watching
i would find him there
        silently weeping
        his head bowed   eyes closed
tears running down his face

and somehow then, even then,
i believed it was more
        gentle
        for him   to him
to leave him there   alone
believing he would have preferred it
        that way
to have that space and time
        to himself

that nearly thirty
        years ago now

and i now already older than
he was then and
eight years older than he lived to be

and again   this evening
a lingering regret
that in those two holiday seasons
him there beside that stereo turntable
i never asked him as he sat there
        alone

where he was then
        and
        what did he see

art festival
for Willa, at Joanne Gervais' two-day 'Art in Kingston' festival – Oct 5 & 6, 2024

an autumn day
an outdoor art festival
in a semi-wooded
area

chipped wood
layered as carpet
        tan and blonde
above the wet earth and
        fading green beneath

rural
casual
3 short rows
        of various artists' tents

a comraderie
connection
        a wooded fragrance
        of wonder
                filling the air

i sat at a small table to host a very very short
version of an intuitive writing workshop
that first morning for Willa - a young teen
just met and coming to it
        sitting there across from me

i offered her a few words about
intuition and writing from that place
shared with her
        reasons   examples
        suggestions   ideas
and told her that before she wrote
she should slowly walk around first
        to explore   to watch

        to sense   absorb
to not think

she looked at me
          as if a bit bewildered
as she walked away

i did not know if she'd really
taken any of it in
had taken it to heart

or if she would write anything at all

she returned to me
well over an hour later

to tell me it was

          and then read me
          her first poem ever

and she was overjoyed

that sight of her
there glowing
          euphoric

and i cannot right now
remember
any better thing that has
happened to me
or in front of me
          in a very long time

and who we are

as i
      or you
exit
whatever is
      that ever-next door

we carry an endless
hope
that we
      loved and cared for
      and perhaps even helped
more people

than we disappointed

revisiting

this morning
a memory arrives
in a softness
and fine mist
      surrounding me in
an as if long awaited
      embrace

this memory from
very   very
long ago

we lived in the country
      then
far away
      from any city
and far enough
      from even
      a tiny town

often
we had to travel
by car
      to anywhere

my son   our son
in that time
decades ago
      just a bit more
      than an infant
not even toddler yet

and always on those drives
strapped into his baby seat
      in the back

quite early on
we noticed

        maybe he then
        5 or 6 months old
whenever we drove
somewhere   anywhere
at some point in it
he would make a hand gesture
        using both hands

he would hold his left
        index finger straight up
and then place his right
        index finger with another
crossways on top of his left

he was not speaking yet
        so too young to ask
and as this kept happening
        more and more often
over at least a couple of months
we were baffled by what
        it was all about

and this only happened
when we were in the car

then one day
as we were driving
a longer drive
        to the city
        to see his doctor in fact
for just a checkup
i could see him in the car's
rearview mirror doing it again

and so
for just a second

i quickly
        but safely   carefully
turned my head around
        to see the direction
        his head was turned
and what he was looking at

                telephone poles

and so
        mystery solved

i believe we even relayed
the whole story
to his pediatrician that morning

but i don't think i
fully understood until
many years later
        perhaps not even
        until today
                just now

Joe was not simply
mimicking
        an image

he was
        speaking to it

        speaking with it
by assembly

learning a deeper language

connecting to

        and creating his world

watching

i sit in a hospital café
looking through its outside walls
these full glass windows

see an older man
having come from inside
out another door and
is now outside
walking past me
toward a parking lot

the one i'm guessing that
he'd parked his car in earlier today

he's carrying
in his left hand   a cane
          horizontally
and under his right arm
two small white bags
          that in very noticeable
          letters say *patient's*
          belongings

i am guessing he's taking
first the bags and cane
to his car
and i'm really only here
for a bit but i am so hoping
to see him quickly
come back from there
to assist his partner
or sibling or mother or father
daughter, or son, grandchild
grandfather, grandmother
friend

       any one of those
and he then
coming back by me
and into the hospital to then
wheel that released patient
in a chair back toward his car

but two things
i did not   do not see –
first
       behind the hospital
       on the other side
       with its engine running
       a funeral director's van

second
       that older man coming back

moon

i'd mentioned as i sat down
in a crowded room
that on my way there
that early evening
            i'd been enthralled
            watching a sliver
of a crescent moon

said to those in that room
while sitting there
            it is my favourite moon

you then right after replied
            there is really only one moon

i said something after

that was purposely silly
            or nonsensical
simply to end that tiny
thread of conversation

that crowded room that evening
was overly vibrant   loud
dozens of conversations
rolling over the tops of each other
            competing for space
with even its much too loud
background music on top of that

that small space that evening
with too many people
too much noise

was not the place to talk
about whispers of the moon

or how fragile it is

that evening she neither
    waxing
    nor waning
but weeping
    instead

around me

there are pictures
  even sounds
of words
  hiding
in the shadows
  and darkness
under the leaves
  of these bushes
ever-near me
as i walk along
  or even stop beside

these
those words that
can neither be seen
nor heard
  by me
  perhaps anyone

but as my legs or
even fingers brush
  atop
  alongside

an almost-sound
  of word
slides out from them
  into me

becoming
  inherited
  absorbed

becoming
  the blood
  and flesh

becoming later
    the ink
    the page

for a moment

i was standing in a sheltered
full glass bus stop

it was tuesday
early to mid morning

and was a minus 20 degrees
counting the wind chill

a young woman came in
probably on her way
to work
          an appointment perhaps

immaculately dressed
beautiful winter coat
showing just a bit of a
a burgundy coloured scarf
          white cashmere sweater
          beneath

black slacks, cut perfectly
          ending just half an inch
          above the heels of
          her shoes

and as she sat down
she reached down the inside left
leg of her pants to its bottom
and with the index finger of
          her right hand
flicked off what might have
been a flake of snow
          or perhaps something else
          picked up on her walk there

that the only thing wrong

    out of place

now fixed

i watched all of this

and that morning i knew
    still fully know

that somewhere
say 200 years from now
someone immaculately dressed
in that time will arrive there
sit down and flick a piece of something
from the bottom of their pant leg

as another person stands there
watching it all
becoming instantly lost
in wonder
    with images of time

    with something they
        can't quite explain

and filled then with
that small idea

    that twinge

of a thing misplaced

    but does not know
      what
      or why

blue
> *after Julia McCarthy's*
> *"All the Names Between"*

blue comes to us
to remind

when
        another colour leaves

or when
        we are looking away

or when
        we believe we don't
        dream in colour

or
        in a ravaging world
        or day
when
        all other colours
        are too much

        or not enough

waking

in the darkness
of this time
when i have neither
fingers nor eyes
        that work
i will say it

i will say it again
        again

        over and over

i will speak into
the night
        not even knowing
        that it is

and i will thank
a world   or a god
for that which is

even that which
        is not

        there is fullness still
                in emptiness
        there is compassion
        even love
                borne of that

i will thank this
      day

          for its magic
its being

for this life
        that is

        what it is

for its openness
its allowances
its breath

        my breath
        our breath

        all breath

i will wait in silence
for as long as it takes

and coming from that
i will ask not
so much for forgiveness
        but acceptance
for my errors
        my mistakes

unfortunate as they
      were

or are

they were never done
intentionally   or in malice
            but
only in and along a journey
            losing
            having lost
                    its way

my humble thanks
to this day
as well for its
ever-inspiration
its courage
integrity
determination

its even regrets

its gentleness
            humility

and again and always
thanking past days and
this day in advance
for its and their remains

and   and   and
all this   all that
has already been said
by those poets
            and others all
greater   better
than i

for i am not yet truly
a poet

but instead
here in the all
of ever-sound
      with the tiniest fraction

      of a mouth
         an ear

i have ever-been listening

listening   listening

    listening
      still

midwinter

as i carry
        in my arms
the assumed weight
of the day
this early morning

there is at least
still a low sun
        on my face

and the wind
        at my back

centre

in its very centre – at its heart
yet still emanating throughout
is any particular thing's
            essence

and in the full all of them
each thing is
            ever-changing

but its original
essence   remains
      untouched

and so
no different
         the acorn

            the oak

there

this day forever
            hanging
on an ever-thread of
            time
will remember itself
as perfectly
            as it was

you and i
here in it now
will each remember
            it
instead
            differently

            temporarily

            and as beautifully
                  imperfect

as each of us are

the muse

i

the muse
i feel
has left this old graveyard

this morning
he no longer seems to
attend to the lichen
        on the tombstones

or tend to the grass between

there is a raven
on a branch above
that calls out to him
        still

that muse's spirit
        gone it seems
but his spirit's spirit i feel
still somehow here

even i can sense

noticed in an almost sweet
scent   wafting by
        hanging
in the air as
breeze's intentions ever-shift

perhaps this muse
once a poet
was ever-drawn to this
particular cemetery
        this place

for a reason

this the muse i have been
visited by each time i'd often
come here to write
the past two dozen years

and always around
          every time

but this time   this visit
absent

perhaps in those years
that muse   always drawn
to this place by a loved one's
remains in this
          earth here below

what drew him here then
made him not stray far

          ever

perhaps today
that muse   that poet
not lost   not gone
instead
          on a journey

some silent sojourn
          a sabbatical
          a walk
away
from this
          ever-sadness
here in the air
wavering   floating
          just above these headstones

here among what's been lost

ii

on the lawn
i sit
here still
in this
      cemetery
same day
same hour
      as if rewound

and here just now

almost hearing footsteps
      behind me

i turn to find
      no one
nothing

nothing but these new
wet footprints
in the grass
      beside
and again that same
scent   and sense
in the air

and i believe

yes
      i believe

the muse
      has returned

ink

again this morning
the pen
       finds a page

its ink always been
       sky blue

but this early morning
for 15 minutes
       at dawn
it
that ink carried instead
the colours
       of sunrise
and splayed them out
in colour transformed

rebirthed

this poem laying
in burgundy
pink   orange
teal   maroon
its ink onto the page

as i will tell you
this backstory and
explain in detail
how the colours of ink
on this page not only
were
but became sunrise's
infinite long threads
spreading from earth's
edge in those original
hues all crossing the land

as far as one could imagine
and attaching themselves
in lines to this poem here
on this page

but I feel
you will not believe me

you
who slept through that sunrise
        this morning

you
who sleep through sunrise
        every day

and you

even now still
        fast asleep
        in this poem

solitude

having lived so long
        alone
        in this place
i fear i am losing

language

at VIA kingston waiting for a train to cobourg

waiting at a train station
feeling a freight train
go thundering by

as it goes
it believes
it is steel
      and strong

i can watch the very top of it
through the small windows
along the uppermost edge
      of an outside wall

the rest of that wall
truly is and believes
it is brick   and stone
and mortar
      and strong

but between that wall
and me
there is a full
windowed wall
      dividing
and adding
a separate space

it is glass
it is invisible
it believes
it is air
      and in that strong

but as i watch
that glass   watching me
it realizes
        it may disguise itself
        as air

but cannot yet pretend
        itself breath

sometimes

sometimes i wonder
if what i write
might be
becoming
     out of favour
     less relevant
     old   archaic
     ancient

that it's lost its place
in general
with a greater   faster
     moving
         world

it's becoming as if
in a way
music
     from a different
     time   ages ago

less popular now

even its package
the book cover
     more landscape than
     vibrant   or
     thrilling   or
     shocking   or
     clever

my words becoming   again
as if analogous to music
     like classical music
with its much smaller
group of followers   admirers

than the popular songs
and rhythms   of the day

and in this i am
not
comparing myself to
        any of those then
        great composers
no

not like beethoven   bach
handel   rachmainov
chopin   mozart
hadyn   brahms
mendelssohn

no
i am less

more like a once young student
of theirs

or not even a student
        but one of those student's
        friends

        or one of their long distant
        cousins

or not even any of those
but instead
in a concert hall
after a classical musical performance
had ended
and all the people there gone home
and all the musicians' chairs
on that stage had been
picked up and
        stacked away

perhaps i then am
the janitor

in that as if infinite
silence
        alone
there sweeping the floor and

        with endless compositions
                songs   music

        never before heard

        ever-and gently-floating about
        in my head

captivated

you will first
notice her out of
the corner of your
      eye

she is watching
something
      something else

she is lost
      engrossed
in what she's seeing
      as she watches

she is locked
      into it

is being pulled
out of any world she
      knows
      has ever known

she is captive to it

she does not know
you are watching
      observing her

she does not
in this very instant
know anything
      that might be
      of this world

but of course
she will return
      she will come
      back to whatever
it was she was doing
before she became
distracted and
entranced by whatever
      it was she is seeing now

and later
she will go about
her days and nights
      like she always
      did
            like everyone else
            does

for awhile

but here right now
just watching
      her
you know already
those few minutes
she had in that
      other place
will come back

      from time to time

will grow

you already know

you already know
those few minutes
she had
        wherever she was
are already taking
        her hand

and changing
her life
        forever

magic

you say
you do not believe
     in magic

nor do you believe
in this

it's too much
     you say

as you recall and scoff at so many
carnival magician acts you'd seen
in the past
     old top hat tricks
          disappearing rabbits
          quickly appearing doves
     decks of cards
          marked or not
     people disappearing
          from a container
          or behind a curtain
     a person in a box
          still alive after
          being sawed in two

     all of that
          superficial
               illusion

beyond all this though

there was
a particular star once
in the sky

it exploded   or imploded
vanished
        from where it was
        10,000 years ago
they say

and even yet they also say
so distant
we will not see it
missing from our night sky
        for another 200 years

that star
with all
that was orbiting it
        and everything upon

gone   gone   gone

but
again tonight
and for the next 200 years
we see it still
        i see it
        you see it
        yes all of us see it still

it is there
        as if right in front of us
still shining

and we
still ever-believing
        only in what we see

and disbelieving   disavowing
        all we can't

farmers market day at the park

a flow of generations
       and circumstance
slow rolling through
this small park today

the oldest of those folks
moving down park's paths here
       subconsciously aware
there will be fewer
of their numbers
       over the weeks
       months   years
       to come
but they consciously seeing
and believing
       something else

the youngest of those here
       babies in carriages
will not remember this
it simply another blip
in that ever-rolling-everything
       rushing by
       every single second

it will all disappear
into an immediate dream

one that for the first time
they will remember
as they walk through this park
80 years on

time

these molasses days

crawl by

    time almost
    frozen in itself

this ever-slow motion
of what
becoming
    is

there again

i believe there
        is a forest
        on an island
on the other side of
        this wide lake
        i cannot see across

i listen to the languages
of the birds

they tell stories
of a vast forest
on this water's other side

perhaps their stories
are poetry though
        and mean also
        something else

perhaps their stories
are music   an old song

a song so old
        before even those trees

almost as old as water
and their melody sprouted
a first tree there
        on the soil beside

perhaps their words
are a dream
a visioning

perhaps the trees
        are not yet there

perhaps this water
before me
        is air instead

perhaps
the only illusion here
                is me

walking by

walking on a back street
finding there a small
run down house

it was as if a small explosion
had happened inside
        perhaps months ago

the door halfway open
blackened edges
slightly tilted
        perhaps partially
        unhinged

i don't know
didn't want to stare
        someone was standing there
        in the yard   between it and me

and it could be like the door
that big window too
        nothing there
        not even frame
as if it had been blown apart
        inside out

and trying not to watch
but watching still
        from the corner of my eye
this middle aged woman
standing there
seeming distant from it all
        even herself

simply wandering back and forth

then in and out
out and in

perhaps she was there
when it happened
     months ago

cannot pull herself away
from the remains
these remnants of what
might have been her home

and perhaps as well
what i'm seeing
is not a person living there
     then or now

but is instead   her ghost

70 years on

flashback images   instants
70 years ago

i might have been 3 or 4

mom, dad, my sister barb, and i
          after our hour long drive
          from my parent's farm
were visiting my dad's parent's
home in the small city where
they had moved after they'd retired
from their own farm
          several years before

i was sitting next to my grandfather
at their dining room table

he slid a big glass bowl over to me
and i pulled out a wrapped small
piece of candy
          my first ever hard candy
          butter-rum

my grandmother later showed me
her basement   her pantry with
all her canned   pickled
          and preserved
vegetables and fruit she'd harvested
from her backyard garden there

and sitting later outside
by myself
          playing with a small
          metallic and slightly
          rusted dump truck
          on the front lawn

all afternoon

i watched the street
in front of their house
and seeing then
what i would have
seen any other day
back in that time
when cars were big
        and plain
and in a whole afternoon
you might see only
        4 or 5 of them go slowly by

and i here now
nearly an old man
sitting in a chair on a lawn still
in a city   and with eyes closed
drawn again this late summer
        afternoon
to those slower
and softer
        times

autumn morning outside

here in this small
    wooded place

i glance around
and pointing at it
let you know what i see

just over there
is a ghost
in a rocking chair
i tell you
as you sit
next to me

you say in return
as you look in that direction
i can see the chair

but i can't see the ghost

i tell you then *the ghost*
    is smiling

but you do not hear me

because
by then
you believe
that even i
    am no longer there

sandcastle

how long
how many years
does wonder last

    its magical silken threads
    attracting   drawing
    us in

before the tides
of logic
    and rules
    protocol
    and standards

    reason
    and commonality

continue to wash
over it
    slowly eroding
    erasing
    chasing it
back into earth

a buried wonder
now but only sand
    flush with the rest

but beneath still
a sandcastle
    hidden
waiting
    there

waiting

waiting
      along this beach
           of time
for a next and
      curious
      joy filled child
to walk by

whispers here

the whispers
call
      in autumn

rattle these brittle
hanging leaves
      even on the stillest
      of day

the softest of voices arrive as if
in waves of themselves

multilayered
multilingual

i stand here in this
coloured forest
beneath what seems a sky
of leaves overhead

it so quiet here
so still

i hear
another whisper
pass alongside me

and but a second later
just ahead
      off a single dry leaf
its echo   there

early morning again – maybe the last

i've been up since long before dawn

wandering streets all morning
        finding nearly no one

maybe two or three times
another wanderer
        in the distance
        here and there
they always farther up the street
or much farther down
        some crossing avenue

i search both ways
turning my head
in each intersection as i pass

i think to myself
perhaps this is the end of times

finally i can see
and find a café's
        doors open
and go inside

no one behind the counter

no one sitting at tables there

but in the next room
        the smaller back room
i hear voices
        many
i turn the corner to look
then walk into

and there again
        no one

there only
multiple stereophonic
        audio speakers
all arranged facing different
        directions

and through them
the sounds of multiple
and over-lapping recordings
        of others
in camaraderie
        and conversation

speakers carrying those
seem as if perfectly
        arranged   and turned
            orchestrated
        choreographed

and perhaps even
compassionately placed
by someone wanting to leave
        something behind
someone who knew what
        was happening

someone

someone
with just enough time
before they too disappeared

moving

everything moves
at its own speed

and with each movement
is slowly letting go
of itself

the old matted remains
of last winter's rotting leaves
are becoming
in the dry late spring sun
almost dust

a conversation loses
itself
       of its own volition

       or with a head turned away

a seed lost in sleep
wakes to newer languages
       and conversations
between wet earth and sun

a breath leaves
a mouth

forgets
from where it came

remembers now
       instead
a different breath
       long ago

       shared

here this morning

in a short distance

a later sunrise
a longer shadow

steam rising from
   a teacup
becomes air

the birds not even
yet awake
   this morning

the only sound
to be heard
   just over there
a humble
appreciative sigh
   of a season
      fully waking

   this first day
   of october

pattern

drawn into and
      now keenly aware

these patterns of clouds
this morning

absolutely the same
as they always are
      exactly 17 hours
          and 11 minutes
      before it rains

and in this hour
these movements of life
      birds in constant song
          chattering
      fervent squirrels having gathered
          now burying their fortunes
      insects endlessly all moving
          scrambling for safety
            and warmth
all in each their own language
of day

i notice as well this morning
how the leaves hang
      differently

how shadows reveal
      their lighter shade

how you this morning again
will see that
      city fox

the one you hadn't seen
for weeks

there are so many worlds
in this one
so many days rolling inside
this hour   this minute

sometimes   i forget
        to fully watch

        to listen

moving into
    for Angela

i remember vividly
moving into this apartment
      now just over 18 years ago

here
a much younger than myself
woman lived in an apartment
      upstairs
she
      an actress
      a gardener
      a gifter
            of things
            of music
            of conversation
            of life
became in that time
a welcoming friend

she only two thirds my age
would become over a short time
an as if younger sister

she lived on the 2nd floor
full big windows to
the south, the east, the west

she pointed out how lucky she was
to live here
      and that i should be now
      by association as well

she could see above the trees
and as i visited her apartment
on one of my first days here

she pointed out
the many church spires
  all but a block
or so away in every direction
even the one to the north
   that we couldn't see

said it made her feel peaceful
   here
and she imagined that i too
should feel the same

i believe i took that then to mean
she was telling me she felt
those spires made her feel welcome

she
an epitome of health
when i moved in
within 2 years developed cancer

   twice

had to move out

and a year later passed away
after a difficult struggle
the second time

i'd always thought she felt
the church spires
were her protection

i wonder now if she felt instead
      not yet knowing the future

but unknowingly sensing it still
they instead
      her salvation
           redemption

in all things
even this

in
each of them

even before
its beginning

its end
was there

already attached

Questions

On a very late-night secluded sidewalk in a city, two people approach each other, coming from opposite directions. There is no one else nearby – or even on that street as far as one could see.

Just as they begin to pass each other -

You can't do that, she says.

What do you mean? I can't do what? he, somewhat startled, replied.

What you were thinking.

Why can't I?

I can't tell you why. I just know.

I don't understand. Are you telling me there's something I shouldn't do?

No, that's not it. That's not strong enough. I'm not simply giving you advice. No, this is more like a warning.

A warning?

Yes, it...it is. A warning. I never pry into other people's lives. But tonight, I am making an exception. I saw you walking, approaching. I've never seen you before and believe you've never seen me. I don't know you. I'd say we just met, here right now, but even that isn't accurate. We haven't met. But as you were walking by, I could sense what you were thinking. So, I told you, 'You can't do that.'

This is crazy. How do you know what I was thinking?

I don't know what you were thinking.

Then, how can you say that I can't do whatever it was I was thinking about?

I can't tell you, really.

What does that mean?

I can't tell, but I can like......sense. Throughout my life, I could often see pieces of other people's futures. Yet with that still, in the past I'd always stopped short of telling others what I thought they should or should not be doing. I figured it wasn't my business. Mostly because - what if my presumptions were wrong? My seeming helpful advice might in the end be depriving them of something that might then lead them somewhere else. And that might be a welcoming and beautiful place. And they there then with wonderful friends. But again, you're my exception. And the first.

So, why are you making me an exception?

Because that sense for me with you was overwhelming. And I felt it would be a big mistake if I didn't tell you. That's why I didn't simply say, 'You shouldn't do that.' I said 'you can't do that.'

But what is it that I can't do?

I don't know. It is what you were thinking.

But what was I thinking?

I don't know.

This is crazy. I should just walk away.

Maybe that's what I'm talking about.

You mean, walking away?

In part, maybe.

Well, I can easily pay no attention to you. Walk away and forget this ever happened.

You can't do that.

What??

You won't be able to do that now. We're too far into this. You won't ever be able to ever forget this conversation.

I'm sure I can.

No, you can't. I know. And I know now then, there are two things you can't do. First, what I just said, And the second - My first words to you as I sensed what you were thinking. And yes, as I did then, I still stand fast in telling you that you can't do that.

I can't do what?!

What you were thinking.

And what was I thinking?

I don't know.

What do you mean, you don't know?

I can't read thoughts.

What does this all mean? You say you can't read my thoughts, but still say that I can't do what I am thinking?

I didn't say I couldn't read your thoughts. I simply said I can't read thoughts – meaning I can't read anyone's thoughts.

This is crazy! I'm walking away.

You won't, now.

Why?

Again, we're too far down this. You're not confused in it or even, really, agitated by it. You're —curious.

That's presumptuous.

No, it's a fact. I'm merely pointing it out.

You mean to tell me I can't leave right now?!

No, I'm just saying you won't leave right now. And I told you why. But I don't see this lasting much longer either.

For God's sake young woman, why did you stop me in the middle of the night on this sidewalk with no one else around to tell me all of this?

Oh, I didn't do it for God's sake, or my sake, or anyone else's really.

You're talking in circles!

No, I'm talking in a straight line. You're listening in circles. I see now, it would have been easier for me to have simply just let you pass and have said nothing.

Well, why didn't you then?

I couldn't. I had to tell you, 'You can't do that.'

Again, with the 'I can't do that.' I can't do what?!!

What you were thinking.

Oh my God, what are you talking about?

OK, let's try it this way. Again, I don't know you. You don't know me. But as you approached, I could see you were deep in thought. There was an absolute blankness in your eyes. An emptiness filled your face. You became ghostlike in it. Your face, ashen. Your body moving as if it were simply robotic, mechanical. There was no life in you. Certainly, no love. And no self-love for sure. And I said, 'You can't do that' meaning you can't think whatever it was you were thinking then. Please don't ever think that way and those kinds of thoughts again! I believe it will lead you to your death. I hope you understand now.

The man looked at her silently for very many minutes. Just stared at her face. And she at his.

He then offered a gentle smile and softly said, *Thank you*, not knowing or having anything else to say.

Facing him, she placed her hands together as if in prayer, tucked them under her chin, and slightly bowed her head acknowledging his thanks. He nodded, smiled again – even a bit truer this time. He then turned to leave. And not directly ahead, but back from where he had come.

A young man on the second floor of the building across the street with the lights on in his apartment behind him, had been watching all of this unfold. He wondered what the two of them had been talking about for so long. He was envisioning so many stories in his head about all he'd seen.

The young woman on the street – glanced up. Saw him there. She smiled. And then continued her walk leaving the street as empty as it was before. As if none of this had ever happened.

dreams

my dreams

i almost never
        remember

perhaps for a few
seconds
        right after i wake
tiny bits and pieces
but even then
        immediately
they're gone

there are a few
        though
where i can sense while
i'm dreaming
        a profound
        familiarity in those

like with a person
or in a gathering
or some settings
        a city
        a town
        a countryside

yes   yes
in those few dreams
it seems i have
        indeed
been there before
        many times

now those
are the ones
i might remember
for a minute or two
or maybe even a bit
        longer
after i open my eyes

and of those
        especially
after i wake
i wonder then
why i keep going
back to those
places or people
        so often

and i question

am i going there
hoping to find
        someone
        something
i recognize
        remember fully

or am i going there
more to see if
        anyone there
        remembers me

waiting for anything

i watched her
in the darkened light

there hadn't been
a word spoken in days

but in the darkness
could still be heard
faint sounds
just outside the door
in hallways
        rolling wheels of carts
        footsteps passing by
        an occasional phone
                in the distance ringing
        a nearby elevator door
                opening
                closing

and here in this room
the only sound
the beeping rhythmic
        heart monitor

a quiet
beep   pause   beep   pause

beep   pause   beep

the prognosis is
        not good
it could be anytime

and it would be then
that the device would go silent
        just long enough

for us to realize it had
and then immediately it
would cry out its long
high-pitched screech

that screech that would
echo through the room
until a nurse or even
a group came in

to quickly check
and then unplug
or reset

i wasn't expecting
to be here

i wasn't expected
to have been here
waiting this long

i've learned sometimes
some spirits
some souls
take a long time
to say goodbye to
the day
the night
the body

that carried them
everywhere

    even this place

and how many times
were those spirits
reluctant to
    give in
    to   let go

but here there is
none of that yet
the monitor still running
no dead silence
no screeching alarm
    no flurry of nurses

and here sitting
all of us together

and in our own silences
our memories reaching back
    to better times
and listening now to that
more gentle   even muffled
and collective
beep pause beep
of each other's
    hearts

on the city bus

very early morning
        winter
sun up
        just barely

i board the bus

in 15 minutes or
less i'll be in
another part of town
and where i need to
be this morning

after scanning my pass
i hurry to a seat before
the bus pulls away

then sitting down
as i quickly look around
there are perhaps
11 or 12 others
sitting here
        with me

all strangers
        I believe
all seeming to have
boarded individually

        except one couple
        across from me
        as they softly talk
            to each other

the rest   all

yes absolutely all
the others are looking
down at their laps
their hand or hands wrapped
around their cellphones
and they there reading
       watching
        tapping or typing
           away

after a few seconds
i look away from them
only to fully appreciate
that i am here
       as they are
surrounded by
essentially glass
       on wheels

and as the bus continues on
with me watching a full
panorama of moving
       landscape
i'm lost in
this transcending
       and transfixing
          world

and i feel better
       because of
       and for it

all the rest
       not looking up
          for a second
       not even once

they
still watching those
tiny screens on their phones

and what was there
would have most likely
still been there
  20 minutes from now

  or even later today

  tomorrow

  next year

but what they missed
outside these windows
as it spread its own life out
and moved there
  absolutely
  and exactly
  as it was
they did not see
and

they
will never have
a chance
to ever
  see it again

something

there's something
about brevity
    that is profoundly
    beautiful

perhaps
that's because
by its very nature
it approaches
    and attempts
    to imitate
        silence

each

on either side of emptiness
is plenitude
      and all three
     each
          a gift

again there is no word for this

we drop small things
            pieces of ourselves
into woven baskets as
we walk through rooms
            of days

we forget them there

we take ourselves out
we weather the storms
            within

we walk through rusted
            fire

just being there   again
            reignites it

10 days on
            it will burn down
            forests
                        within us

we will be the only ones
to notice each our own
            smoke

we will not talk about it

we will even look away
if someone else mentions it
            in themselves

we fear they will see
in our eyes
            the fire   the smoke

the ashes
that trail we leave
and have left behind
        both within us
        and beyond

we are told that somewhere
            out there
is a lake

            it might even be
            just around this next corner
                    we tell ourselves

that place where we can
            cleanse it all

            smother the fire
            knock down the smoke
            turn ash back into earth

                still we have not yet
                    seen that lake

            we never seem
                    to find it

            we wander on

but the spirits
    the voices

    the poets
tell me
    it is there

so
    i must
        believe

Bruce Kauffman lives in Kingston, Ontario and is a poet, editor, intuitive workshop facilitator, and promoter. His written work has appeared in anthologies and journals, two chapbooks, and this now his sixth collection of poetry. His most recent prior to this was still arriving, published by Wet Ink Books in 2023. He continues to host a monthly open mic reading series called 'and the journey continues' that began in 2009. And, since 2010, still produces and hosts the weekly radio show called 'finding a voice' on CFRC 101.9fm. Bruce, in 2015, began the annual summer outdoor poetry series, Poets @ Artfest, in conjunction with Artfest Kingston, and has organized and hosted it each summer since.

A Review Essay of Bruce Kauffman's
ever-crossings

Prof. Miguel Ángel Olivé Iglesias. MSc
Author, Poet, Writer, Editor, Translator, Reviewer
General VP of the Canada Caribbean Literary Alliance

My eyes travel along fifty-one poems by Bruce Kauffman in his 2025 Wet Ink Books *ever-crossings*. I have read and reviewed Kauffman before, always admiring his resourcefulness with the language to forge a universe of his own as he arranges and rearranges words and stanzas, semantics and structure, to come up with his engaging poems. About his earlier work, I have written that he "*captures and enraptures all in one for its deeply meditative character.*" This constant remains much alive in *ever-crossings.*

In his first piece, "once," he tells us:

> *once there was*
> > *a day*
> > *or a moment*
> > *or a person*
> > *a thing*
> *so brilliant*
> *so perfect*
> *it could never*
> > *happen again*

> *and then it did*

Kauffman invites to a reinvention of what cannot "*happen again.*" Notice how he leaves an altogether necessary space between the first fragment and the line that ends the poem. This empty space might look cursorily awkward yet its connotation adds to the power of what the poet is proposing, a realistic reenacting of what seems to be and impossibility turned into a "*then it did.*" Therefore, for me the in-between void means the passing of time, the unstoppable cycle of life renewing itself, the miracle of the possible and, above all, the idea of expectation in a new beginning that wondrously blossoms.

Be it nature *per se* or people (but we are nature too!), life re-happens. In it, the glory of moving forward, of rebirth. In Canadian Poet Laureate Richard Grove's words, "Kauffman's language is deceptively simple yet layered with philosophical depth, guiding readers toward a renewed awareness of presence and possibility…" Voilà! The poem is simple; nonetheless, therein we find a truth that touches us.

Now read the following fragment in Kauffman's "questions again":

> *i ask questions*
> *in the dark*
>
> *alone*
>
> *not even sure if*
> *anyone is listening*
>
> *i ask also*
> *for breath*
>   *and have been*
>   *given that so far*
>
> *so perhaps*
>   *someone is*

The poet uses the interesting "*perhaps.*" Indeed, he realises that in the immense territory of life, openness of mind, gratitude for what we have, a bit of temperance and going onward, very much balance our existence—at least his. About previous poems by Kauffman, I have stated that there is an "... *optimistic touch and plants in us the sensation that the poet speaks in terms of progression not of only an ordinary phenomenon but also of the whole conception of existence and the attitude required to confront it.*" It is manifest at this point of my analyses that these views mark Kauffman's style and perspective in writing.

Poem three, "on writing poetry," is a fine piece where we perceive his insightfulness into creative writing and we are pleasingly impressed by his sentience and his keenness to detect where the muses are. Read his introductory lines:

> *you will not write*
> *your best poems*
> > *on paper*
>
> *especially not*
> > *a computer*

He is absolutely certain inspirational themes are in front of us; they come from reality, and it is in the poet's acuity—and heart—to *see* (fragment):

> *you will seemingly*
> *write those instead*
>
> *with invisible ink*
> > *on the backs of wild*
> > *horses and ponies*
>
> *or in a patterned*
> *remnant of tea leaves*
> > *on the feathered*
> > *tail of a dove*

Notice again the stylistically intentional and clever use of line spaces. They give readers time to take in the significance of each creature, thing, component, all of which are in nature. The line spaces Kauffman exploits so masterfully are wings of silence communicating as emotionally as words themselves. Pablo Neruda wrote, "… *the word is a wing of silence*." Well, let us reverse that phrase and say that in Kauffman "silence is the other wing of the word."

The poet announces the wondrous symbiotic bond occurring between poet and surroundings, a bond that explains the how and the why of poetry. He addresses the creative process, the act of writing poetry unquestionably connected to what is around the writer.

A highly heart-moving and symbolic poem comes to me with "waking." If I were to summarise the book's essence and the poet's writing and living ethics, I would choose this poem. Its first two lines read, "*in the darkness / of this time*". They describe a timeless condition of human existence Kauffman compacts and offers to the readers to mull over. Their meaning echoes beyond the poet's personal circumstances in which he writes the poem and can be applied to any actual situation. Then the poet deploys his full repertoire of what it is needed to stand and soldier on:

> *i will speak into*
> *the night*
> > *not even knowing*
> > *that it is*
>
> *and i will thank*
> *a world   or a god*
> *for that which is*
>
> *even that which*
> > *is not*

In his poems, Kauffman directs towards us "*timeless mirrors reflecting a world that belongs to everyone, a world stripped down to its spiritual bones*" as Jason Heroux says. We are witnesses of that in his other books and in *ever-crossings*.

Everydayness, the go-and-go, the common things of life we might call routines is captured by Kauffman in his last poem, "again there is no word for this." Consider these lines:

we drop small things
pieces of ourselves
into woven baskets as
we walk through rooms
of days

we forget them there

In them we observe not only literal commonplace in the actions but also the additional metaphorical element in "*pieces of ourselves*" and "*rooms of days*." The writer inhabits the days; they open and close for him. Kauffman entertains the thought of a possible "*cleansing*" typified in a lake:

we are told that somewhere
out there
is a lake

it might even be
just around this next corner
we tell ourselves

that place where we can
cleanse it all

And he positively adheres to hope in stanzas that give solid concretion to faith understood as "*firm belief in something for which there is no proof, something that is believed especially with strong conviction*." (*Merriam-Webster Collegiate Dictionary*):

still we have not yet
seen that lake

we never seem
to find it

we wander on
but the spirits
the voices

the poets
　tell me
　　it is there

so
　i must
　　believe

Bruce Kauffman believes, he has faith—he treasures *hope*. This is the poet, this is *ever-crossings*, these are the lines he organises so purposefully in order to blend form and content, configuration and meaning into a substantial message aiming at nothing less than believing, because he *must believe*—and we are summoned to believe alongside him! Read *ever-crossings*, Bruce Kauffman's 2025 book published by Wet Ink Books. Come to the meeting point where possibilities cross and re-cross in the endless timeline of existing.

www.ingramcontent.com/pod-product-compliance
Lightning Source LLC
Chambersburg PA
CBHW051217120626
46547CB00013B/1390